Abatron **Logbooks**

LOGBOOK OWNER INFORMATION

NAME	
ADDRESS	
PHONE NUMBER	
EMAIL	
LOGBOOK NUMBER #	

INSURANCE INFORMATION

COMPANY		POLICY NUMBER	
START DATE		END DATE	
PRICE		COVERAGE TYPE	
CONTACT NUMBER		NOTES	
EMAIL			
WEBSITE			

COMPANY		POLICY NUMBER	
START DATE		END DATE	
PRICE		COVERAGE TYPE	
CONTACT NUMBER		NOTES	
EMAIL			
WEBSITE			

COMPANY		POLICY NUMBER	
START DATE		END DATE	
PRICE		COVERAGE TYPE	
CONTACT NUMBER		NOTES	
EMAIL			
WEBSITE			

INSURANCE INFORMATION

COMPANY		POLICY NUMBER	
START DATE		END DATE	
PRICE		COVERAGE TYPE	
CONTACT NUMBER			
EMAIL		NOTES	
WEBSITE			

COMPANY		POLICY NUMBER	
START DATE		END DATE	
PRICE		COVERAGE TYPE	
CONTACT NUMBER			
EMAIL		NOTES	
WEBSITE			

COMPANY		POLICY NUMBER	
START DATE		END DATE	
PRICE		COVERAGE TYPE	
CONTACT NUMBER			
EMAIL		NOTES	
WEBSITE			

FIREARM NAME:

FIREARM TYPE			
☐ HANDGUN	☐ SHOTGUN	☐ AIR GUN	☐ SMG
☐ RIFLE	☐ PISTOL	☐ OTHER _____	

SERIAL NUMBER		MANUFACTURER	
MODEL / TYPE		CALIBER	
WEIGHT		CAPACITY	
BARREL LENGTH		BARREL TYPE	
ACTION		IDENTIFIERS	
ALTERATIONS		OTHER NOTES	
REPAIRS			

📷

ACQUISITION & DISPOSITION INFORMATION

PURCHASED FROM		DATE	
ADDRESS			
ID NUMBER		DOB	
CONDITION		PRICE	
PURCHASE DETAILS			

SOLD TO		DATE	
ADDRESS			
ID NUMBER		DOB	
CONDITION		PRICE	
SALE DETAILS			

OTHER NOTES	

FIREARM NAME:

02

FIREARM TYPE

- ☐ HANDGUN
- ☐ SHOTGUN
- ☐ AIR GUN
- ☐ SMG
- ☐ RIFLE
- ☐ PISTOL
- ☐ OTHER _____

SERIAL NUMBER		**MANUFACTURER**	
MODEL / TYPE		**CALIBER**	
WEIGHT		**CAPACITY**	
BARREL LENGTH		**BARREL TYPE**	
ACTION		**IDENTIFIERS**	
ALTERATIONS		**OTHER NOTES**	
REPAIRS			

ACQUISITION & DISPOSITION INFORMATION

PURCHASED FROM		DATE	
ADDRESS			
ID NUMBER		DOB	
CONDITION		PRICE	
PURCHASE DETAILS			

SOLD TO		DATE	
ADDRESS			
ID NUMBER		DOB	
CONDITION		PRICE	
SALE DETAILS			

OTHER NOTES	

FIREARM NAME:

FIREARM TYPE			
☐ HANDGUN	☐ SHOTGUN	☐ AIR GUN	☐ SMG
☐ RIFLE	☐ PISTOL	☐ OTHER _____	

SERIAL NUMBER		MANUFACTURER	
MODEL / TYPE		CALIBER	
WEIGHT		CAPACITY	
BARREL LENGTH		BARREL TYPE	
ACTION		IDENTIFIERS	
ALTERATIONS		OTHER NOTES	
REPAIRS			

ACQUISITION & DISPOSITION INFORMATION

PURCHASED FROM		DATE	
ADDRESS			
ID NUMBER		DOB	
CONDITION		PRICE	
PURCHASE DETAILS			

SOLD TO		DATE	
ADDRESS			
ID NUMBER		DOB	
CONDITION		PRICE	
SALE DETAILS			

OTHER NOTES	

FIREARM NAME:

FIREARM TYPE		

☐ HANDGUN   ☐ SHOTGUN   ☐ AIR GUN   ☐ SMG

☐ RIFLE   ☐ PISTOL   ☐ OTHER _____

SERIAL NUMBER		**MANUFACTURER**	
MODEL / TYPE		**CALIBER**	
WEIGHT		**CAPACITY**	
BARREL LENGTH		**BARREL TYPE**	
ACTION		**IDENTIFIERS**	
ALTERATIONS		**OTHER NOTES**	
REPAIRS			

ACQUISITION & DISPOSITION INFORMATION

PURCHASED FROM		DATE	
ADDRESS			
ID NUMBER		DOB	
CONDITION		PRICE	
PURCHASE DETAILS			

SOLD TO		DATE	
ADDRESS			
ID NUMBER		DOB	
CONDITION		PRICE	
SALE DETAILS			

OTHER NOTES	

FIREARM NAME:	05

FIREARM TYPE			
☐ HANDGUN	☐ SHOTGUN	☐ AIR GUN	☐ SMG
☐ RIFLE	☐ PISTOL	☐ OTHER _____	

SERIAL NUMBER		MANUFACTURER	
MODEL / TYPE		CALIBER	
WEIGHT		CAPACITY	
BARREL LENGTH		BARREL TYPE	
ACTION		IDENTIFIERS	
ALTERATIONS		OTHER NOTES	
REPAIRS			

📷

ACQUISITION & DISPOSITION INFORMATION

PURCHASED FROM		DATE	
ADDRESS			
ID NUMBER		DOB	
CONDITION		PRICE	
PURCHASE DETAILS			

SOLD TO		DATE	
ADDRESS			
ID NUMBER		DOB	
CONDITION		PRICE	
SALE DETAILS			

OTHER NOTES	

FIREARM NAME:

FIREARM TYPE			
☐ HANDGUN	☐ SHOTGUN	☐ AIR GUN	☐ SMG
☐ RIFLE	☐ PISTOL	☐ OTHER _____	

SERIAL NUMBER		MANUFACTURER	
MODEL / TYPE		CALIBER	
WEIGHT		CAPACITY	
BARREL LENGTH		BARREL TYPE	
ACTION		IDENTIFIERS	
ALTERATIONS		OTHER NOTES	
REPAIRS			

ACQUISITION & DISPOSITION INFORMATION

PURCHASED FROM		DATE	
ADDRESS			
ID NUMBER		DOB	
CONDITION		PRICE	
PURCHASE DETAILS			

SOLD TO		DATE	
ADDRESS			
ID NUMBER		DOB	
CONDITION		PRICE	
SALE DETAILS			

OTHER NOTES	

FIREARM NAME:

FIREARM TYPE

☐ HANDGUN   ☐ SHOTGUN   ☐ AIR GUN   ☐ SMG

☐ RIFLE   ☐ PISTOL   ☐ OTHER _____

SERIAL NUMBER		MANUFACTURER	
MODEL / TYPE		CALIBER	
WEIGHT		CAPACITY	
BARREL LENGTH		BARREL TYPE	
ACTION		IDENTIFIERS	
ALTERATIONS		OTHER NOTES	
REPAIRS			

ACQUISITION & DISPOSITION INFORMATION

PURCHASED FROM		DATE	
ADDRESS			
ID NUMBER		DOB	
CONDITION		PRICE	
PURCHASE DETAILS			

SOLD TO		DATE	
ADDRESS			
ID NUMBER		DOB	
CONDITION		PRICE	
SALE DETAILS			

OTHER NOTES	

FIREARM NAME:

FIREARM TYPE			
☐ HANDGUN	☐ SHOTGUN	☐ AIR GUN	☐ SMG
☐ RIFLE	☐ PISTOL	☐ OTHER _____	

SERIAL NUMBER		MANUFACTURER	
MODEL / TYPE		CALIBER	
WEIGHT		CAPACITY	
BARREL LENGTH		BARREL TYPE	
ACTION		IDENTIFIERS	
ALTERATIONS		OTHER NOTES	
REPAIRS			

ACQUISITION & DISPOSITION INFORMATION

PURCHASED FROM		DATE	
ADDRESS			
ID NUMBER		DOB	
CONDITION		PRICE	
PURCHASE DETAILS			

SOLD TO		DATE	
ADDRESS			
ID NUMBER		DOB	
CONDITION		PRICE	
SALE DETAILS			

OTHER NOTES	

FIREARM NAME:

FIREARM TYPE

- ☐ HANDGUN
- ☐ RIFLE
- ☐ SHOTGUN
- ☐ PISTOL
- ☐ AIR GUN
- ☐ OTHER _____
- ☐ SMG

SERIAL NUMBER		**MANUFACTURER**	
MODEL / TYPE		**CALIBER**	
WEIGHT		**CAPACITY**	
BARREL LENGTH		**BARREL TYPE**	
ACTION		**IDENTIFIERS**	
ALTERATIONS		**OTHER NOTES**	
REPAIRS			

ACQUISITION & DISPOSITION INFORMATION

PURCHASED FROM		DATE	
ADDRESS			
ID NUMBER		DOB	
CONDITION		PRICE	
PURCHASE DETAILS			

SOLD TO		DATE	
ADDRESS			
ID NUMBER		DOB	
CONDITION		PRICE	
SALE DETAILS			

OTHER NOTES	

FIREARM NAME:

FIREARM TYPE

☐ HANDGUN   ☐ SHOTGUN   ☐ AIR GUN   ☐ SMG

☐ RIFLE   ☐ PISTOL   ☐ OTHER _____

SERIAL NUMBER		**MANUFACTURER**	
MODEL / TYPE		**CALIBER**	
WEIGHT		**CAPACITY**	
BARREL LENGTH		**BARREL TYPE**	
ACTION		**IDENTIFIERS**	
ALTERATIONS		**OTHER NOTES**	
REPAIRS			

ACQUISITION & DISPOSITION INFORMATION

PURCHASED FROM		DATE	
ADDRESS			
ID NUMBER		DOB	
CONDITION		PRICE	
PURCHASE DETAILS			

SOLD TO		DATE	
ADDRESS			
ID NUMBER		DOB	
CONDITION		PRICE	
SALE DETAILS			

OTHER NOTES	

FIREARM NAME:

11

FIREARM TYPE			
☐ HANDGUN	☐ SHOTGUN	☐ AIR GUN	☐ SMG
☐ RIFLE	☐ PISTOL	☐ OTHER _____	

SERIAL NUMBER		**MANUFACTURER**	
MODEL / TYPE		**CALIBER**	
WEIGHT		**CAPACITY**	
BARREL LENGTH		**BARREL TYPE**	
ACTION		**IDENTIFIERS**	
ALTERATIONS		**OTHER NOTES**	
REPAIRS			

ACQUISITION & DISPOSITION INFORMATION

PURCHASED FROM		DATE	
ADDRESS			
ID NUMBER		DOB	
CONDITION		PRICE	
PURCHASE DETAILS			

SOLD TO		DATE	
ADDRESS			
ID NUMBER		DOB	
CONDITION		PRICE	
SALE DETAILS			

OTHER NOTES	

FIREARM NAME: 12

FIREARM TYPE			
☐ HANDGUN	☐ SHOTGUN	☐ AIR GUN	☐ SMG
☐ RIFLE	☐ PISTOL	☐ OTHER _____	

SERIAL NUMBER		MANUFACTURER	
MODEL / TYPE		CALIBER	
WEIGHT		CAPACITY	
BARREL LENGTH		BARREL TYPE	
ACTION		IDENTIFIERS	
ALTERATIONS		OTHER NOTES	
REPAIRS			

ACQUISITION & DISPOSITION INFORMATION

PURCHASED FROM		DATE	
ADDRESS			
ID NUMBER		DOB	
CONDITION		PRICE	
PURCHASE DETAILS			

SOLD TO		DATE	
ADDRESS			
ID NUMBER		DOB	
CONDITION		PRICE	
SALE DETAILS			

OTHER NOTES	

FIREARM NAME: | 13

FIREARM TYPE			
☐ HANDGUN	☐ SHOTGUN	☐ AIR GUN	☐ SMG
☐ RIFLE	☐ PISTOL	☐ OTHER _____	

SERIAL NUMBER		**MANUFACTURER**	
MODEL / TYPE		**CALIBER**	
WEIGHT		**CAPACITY**	
BARREL LENGTH		**BARREL TYPE**	
ACTION		**IDENTIFIERS**	
ALTERATIONS		**OTHER NOTES**	
REPAIRS			

ACQUISITION & DISPOSITION INFORMATION

PURCHASED FROM		DATE	
ADDRESS			
ID NUMBER		DOB	
CONDITION		PRICE	
PURCHASE DETAILS			

SOLD TO		DATE	
ADDRESS			
ID NUMBER		DOB	
CONDITION		PRICE	
SALE DETAILS			

OTHER NOTES	

FIREARM NAME:

FIREARM TYPE			
☐ HANDGUN	☐ SHOTGUN	☐ AIR GUN	☐ SMG
☐ RIFLE	☐ PISTOL	☐ OTHER _____	

SERIAL NUMBER		**MANUFACTURER**	
MODEL / TYPE		**CALIBER**	
WEIGHT		**CAPACITY**	
BARREL LENGTH		**BARREL TYPE**	
ACTION		**IDENTIFIERS**	
ALTERATIONS		**OTHER NOTES**	
REPAIRS			

ACQUISITION & DISPOSITION INFORMATION

PURCHASED FROM		DATE	
ADDRESS			
ID NUMBER		DOB	
CONDITION		PRICE	
PURCHASE DETAILS			

SOLD TO		DATE	
ADDRESS			
ID NUMBER		DOB	
CONDITION		PRICE	
SALE DETAILS			

OTHER NOTES	

FIREARM NAME:

FIREARM TYPE			
☐ HANDGUN	☐ SHOTGUN	☐ AIR GUN	☐ SMG
☐ RIFLE	☐ PISTOL	☐ OTHER _____	

SERIAL NUMBER		MANUFACTURER	
MODEL / TYPE		CALIBER	
WEIGHT		CAPACITY	
BARREL LENGTH		BARREL TYPE	
ACTION		IDENTIFIERS	
ALTERATIONS		OTHER NOTES	
REPAIRS			

ACQUISITION & DISPOSITION INFORMATION

PURCHASED FROM		DATE	
ADDRESS			
ID NUMBER		DOB	
CONDITION		PRICE	
PURCHASE DETAILS			

SOLD TO		DATE	
ADDRESS			
ID NUMBER		DOB	
CONDITION		PRICE	
SALE DETAILS			

OTHER NOTES	

FIREARM NAME:

FIREARM TYPE

- ☐ HANDGUN
- ☐ RIFLE
- ☐ SHOTGUN
- ☐ PISTOL
- ☐ AIR GUN
- ☐ OTHER _____
- ☐ SMG

SERIAL NUMBER		MANUFACTURER	
MODEL / TYPE		CALIBER	
WEIGHT		CAPACITY	
BARREL LENGTH		BARREL TYPE	
ACTION		IDENTIFIERS	
ALTERATIONS		OTHER NOTES	
REPAIRS			

ACQUISITION & DISPOSITION INFORMATION

PURCHASED FROM		DATE	
ADDRESS			
ID NUMBER		DOB	
CONDITION		PRICE	
PURCHASE DETAILS			

SOLD TO		DATE	
ADDRESS			
ID NUMBER		DOB	
CONDITION		PRICE	
SALE DETAILS			

OTHER NOTES	

FIREARM NAME: 17

FIREARM TYPE			
☐ HANDGUN	☐ SHOTGUN	☐ AIR GUN	☐ SMG
☐ RIFLE	☐ PISTOL	☐ OTHER _____	

SERIAL NUMBER		MANUFACTURER	
MODEL / TYPE		CALIBER	
WEIGHT		CAPACITY	
BARREL LENGTH		BARREL TYPE	
ACTION		IDENTIFIERS	
ALTERATIONS		OTHER NOTES	
REPAIRS			

ACQUISITION & DISPOSITION INFORMATION

PURCHASED FROM		DATE	
ADDRESS			
ID NUMBER		DOB	
CONDITION		PRICE	
PURCHASE DETAILS			

SOLD TO		DATE	
ADDRESS			
ID NUMBER		DOB	
CONDITION		PRICE	
SALE DETAILS			

OTHER NOTES	

FIREARM NAME:

18

FIREARM TYPE			
☐ HANDGUN	☐ SHOTGUN	☐ AIR GUN	☐ SMG
☐ RIFLE	☐ PISTOL	☐ OTHER _____	

SERIAL NUMBER		MANUFACTURER	
MODEL / TYPE		CALIBER	
WEIGHT		CAPACITY	
BARREL LENGTH		BARREL TYPE	
ACTION		IDENTIFIERS	
ALTERATIONS		OTHER NOTES	
REPAIRS			

ACQUISITION & DISPOSITION INFORMATION

PURCHASED FROM		DATE	
ADDRESS			
ID NUMBER		DOB	
CONDITION		PRICE	
PURCHASE DETAILS			

SOLD TO		DATE	
ADDRESS			
ID NUMBER		DOB	
CONDITION		PRICE	
SALE DETAILS			

OTHER NOTES	

FIREARM NAME: | 19

FIREARM TYPE			
☐ HANDGUN	☐ SHOTGUN	☐ AIR GUN	☐ SMG
☐ RIFLE	☐ PISTOL	☐ OTHER _____	

SERIAL NUMBER		MANUFACTURER	
MODEL / TYPE		CALIBER	
WEIGHT		CAPACITY	
BARREL LENGTH		BARREL TYPE	
ACTION		IDENTIFIERS	
ALTERATIONS		OTHER NOTES	
REPAIRS			

ACQUISITION & DISPOSITION INFORMATION

PURCHASED FROM		DATE	
ADDRESS			
ID NUMBER		DOB	
CONDITION		PRICE	
PURCHASE DETAILS			

SOLD TO		DATE	
ADDRESS			
ID NUMBER		DOB	
CONDITION		PRICE	
SALE DETAILS			

OTHER NOTES	

FIREARM NAME:

20

FIREARM TYPE

☐ HANDGUN	☐ SHOTGUN	☐ AIR GUN	☐ SMG
☐ RIFLE	☐ PISTOL	☐ OTHER _____	

SERIAL NUMBER		**MANUFACTURER**	
MODEL / TYPE		**CALIBER**	
WEIGHT		**CAPACITY**	
BARREL LENGTH		**BARREL TYPE**	
ACTION		**IDENTIFIERS**	
ALTERATIONS		**OTHER NOTES**	
REPAIRS			

ACQUISITION & DISPOSITION INFORMATION

PURCHASED FROM		DATE	
ADDRESS			
ID NUMBER		DOB	
CONDITION		PRICE	
PURCHASE DETAILS			

SOLD TO		DATE	
ADDRESS			
ID NUMBER		DOB	
CONDITION		PRICE	
SALE DETAILS			

OTHER NOTES	

FIREARM NAME:

FIREARM TYPE

☐ HANDGUN	☐ SHOTGUN	☐ AIR GUN	☐ SMG
☐ RIFLE	☐ PISTOL	☐ OTHER _____	

SERIAL NUMBER		**MANUFACTURER**	
MODEL / TYPE		**CALIBER**	
WEIGHT		**CAPACITY**	
BARREL LENGTH		**BARREL TYPE**	
ACTION		**IDENTIFIERS**	
ALTERATIONS		**OTHER NOTES**	
REPAIRS			

ACQUISITION & DISPOSITION INFORMATION

PURCHASED FROM		DATE	
ADDRESS			
ID NUMBER		DOB	
CONDITION		PRICE	
PURCHASE DETAILS			

SOLD TO		DATE	
ADDRESS			
ID NUMBER		DOB	
CONDITION		PRICE	
SALE DETAILS			

OTHER NOTES	

FIREARM NAME:

FIREARM TYPE			
☐ HANDGUN	☐ SHOTGUN	☐ AIR GUN	☐ SMG
☐ RIFLE	☐ PISTOL	☐ OTHER _____	

SERIAL NUMBER		MANUFACTURER	
MODEL / TYPE		CALIBER	
WEIGHT		CAPACITY	
BARREL LENGTH		BARREL TYPE	
ACTION		IDENTIFIERS	
ALTERATIONS		OTHER NOTES	
REPAIRS			

ACQUISITION & DISPOSITION INFORMATION

PURCHASED FROM		DATE	
ADDRESS			
ID NUMBER		DOB	
CONDITION		PRICE	
PURCHASE DETAILS			

SOLD TO		DATE	
ADDRESS			
ID NUMBER		DOB	
CONDITION		PRICE	
SALE DETAILS			

OTHER NOTES	

FIREARM NAME: | 23

FIREARM TYPE			
☐ HANDGUN	☐ SHOTGUN	☐ AIR GUN	☐ SMG
☐ RIFLE	☐ PISTOL	☐ OTHER _____	

SERIAL NUMBER		MANUFACTURER	
MODEL / TYPE		CALIBER	
WEIGHT		CAPACITY	
BARREL LENGTH		BARREL TYPE	
ACTION		IDENTIFIERS	
ALTERATIONS		OTHER NOTES	
REPAIRS			

ACQUISITION & DISPOSITION INFORMATION

PURCHASED FROM		DATE	
ADDRESS			
ID NUMBER		DOB	
CONDITION		PRICE	
PURCHASE DETAILS			

SOLD TO		DATE	
ADDRESS			
ID NUMBER		DOB	
CONDITION		PRICE	
SALE DETAILS			

OTHER NOTES	

FIREARM TYPE			
☐ HANDGUN	☐ SHOTGUN	☐ AIR GUN	☐ SMG
☐ RIFLE	☐ PISTOL	☐ OTHER _____	

SERIAL NUMBER		**MANUFACTURER**	
MODEL / TYPE		**CALIBER**	
WEIGHT		**CAPACITY**	
BARREL LENGTH		**BARREL TYPE**	
ACTION		**IDENTIFIERS**	
ALTERATIONS		**OTHER NOTES**	
REPAIRS			

ACQUISITION & DISPOSITION INFORMATION

PURCHASED FROM		DATE	
ADDRESS			
ID NUMBER		DOB	
CONDITION		PRICE	
PURCHASE DETAILS			

SOLD TO		DATE	
ADDRESS			
ID NUMBER		DOB	
CONDITION		PRICE	
SALE DETAILS			

OTHER NOTES	

FIREARM NAME:

FIREARM TYPE			
☐ HANDGUN	☐ SHOTGUN	☐ AIR GUN	☐ SMG
☐ RIFLE	☐ PISTOL	☐ OTHER _____	

SERIAL NUMBER		**MANUFACTURER**	
MODEL / TYPE		**CALIBER**	
WEIGHT		**CAPACITY**	
BARREL LENGTH		**BARREL TYPE**	
ACTION		**IDENTIFIERS**	
ALTERATIONS		**OTHER NOTES**	
REPAIRS			

ACQUISITION & DISPOSITION INFORMATION

PURCHASED FROM		DATE	
ADDRESS			
ID NUMBER		DOB	
CONDITION		PRICE	
PURCHASE DETAILS			

SOLD TO		DATE	
ADDRESS			
ID NUMBER		DOB	
CONDITION		PRICE	
SALE DETAILS			

OTHER NOTES	

FIREARM NAME: 26

FIREARM TYPE			
☐ HANDGUN	☐ SHOTGUN	☐ AIR GUN	☐ SMG
☐ RIFLE	☐ PISTOL	☐ OTHER _____	

SERIAL NUMBER		**MANUFACTURER**	
MODEL / TYPE		**CALIBER**	
WEIGHT		**CAPACITY**	
BARREL LENGTH		**BARREL TYPE**	
ACTION		**IDENTIFIERS**	
ALTERATIONS		**OTHER NOTES**	
REPAIRS			

ACQUISITION & DISPOSITION INFORMATION

PURCHASED FROM		DATE	
ADDRESS			
ID NUMBER		DOB	
CONDITION		PRICE	
PURCHASE DETAILS			

SOLD TO		DATE	
ADDRESS			
ID NUMBER		DOB	
CONDITION		PRICE	
SALE DETAILS			

OTHER NOTES	

FIREARM NAME:

FIREARM TYPE

| ☐ HANDGUN | ☐ SHOTGUN | ☐ AIR GUN | ☐ SMG |
| ☐ RIFLE | ☐ PISTOL | ☐ OTHER _____ | |

SERIAL NUMBER		**MANUFACTURER**	
MODEL / TYPE		**CALIBER**	
WEIGHT		**CAPACITY**	
BARREL LENGTH		**BARREL TYPE**	
ACTION		**IDENTIFIERS**	
ALTERATIONS		**OTHER NOTES**	
REPAIRS			

ACQUISITION & DISPOSITION INFORMATION

PURCHASED FROM		DATE	
ADDRESS			
ID NUMBER		DOB	
CONDITION		PRICE	
PURCHASE DETAILS			

SOLD TO		DATE	
ADDRESS			
ID NUMBER		DOB	
CONDITION		PRICE	
SALE DETAILS			

OTHER NOTES	

FIREARM NAME: 28

FIREARM TYPE			
☐ HANDGUN	☐ SHOTGUN	☐ AIR GUN	☐ SMG
☐ RIFLE	☐ PISTOL	☐ OTHER _____	

SERIAL NUMBER		MANUFACTURER	
MODEL / TYPE		CALIBER	
WEIGHT		CAPACITY	
BARREL LENGTH		BARREL TYPE	
ACTION		IDENTIFIERS	
ALTERATIONS		OTHER NOTES	
REPAIRS			

ACQUISITION & DISPOSITION INFORMATION

PURCHASED FROM		DATE	
ADDRESS			
ID NUMBER		DOB	
CONDITION		PRICE	
PURCHASE DETAILS			

SOLD TO		DATE	
ADDRESS			
ID NUMBER		DOB	
CONDITION		PRICE	
SALE DETAILS			

OTHER NOTES	

FIREARM NAME:

FIREARM TYPE

☐ HANDGUN   ☐ SHOTGUN   ☐ AIR GUN   ☐ SMG
☐ RIFLE   ☐ PISTOL   ☐ OTHER _____

SERIAL NUMBER		MANUFACTURER	
MODEL / TYPE		CALIBER	
WEIGHT		CAPACITY	
BARREL LENGTH		BARREL TYPE	
ACTION		IDENTIFIERS	
ALTERATIONS		OTHER NOTES	
REPAIRS			

ACQUISITION & DISPOSITION INFORMATION

PURCHASED FROM		DATE	
ADDRESS			
ID NUMBER		DOB	
CONDITION		PRICE	
PURCHASE DETAILS			

SOLD TO		DATE	
ADDRESS			
ID NUMBER		DOB	
CONDITION		PRICE	
SALE DETAILS			

OTHER NOTES	

FIREARM NAME:

FIREARM TYPE

☐ HANDGUN	☐ SHOTGUN	☐ AIR GUN	☐ SMG
☐ RIFLE	☐ PISTOL	☐ OTHER _____	

SERIAL NUMBER		MANUFACTURER	
MODEL / TYPE		CALIBER	
WEIGHT		CAPACITY	
BARREL LENGTH		BARREL TYPE	
ACTION		IDENTIFIERS	
ALTERATIONS		OTHER NOTES	
REPAIRS			

ACQUISITION & DISPOSITION INFORMATION

PURCHASED FROM		DATE	
ADDRESS			
ID NUMBER		DOB	
CONDITION		PRICE	
PURCHASE DETAILS			

SOLD TO		DATE	
ADDRESS			
ID NUMBER		DOB	
CONDITION		PRICE	
SALE DETAILS			

OTHER NOTES	

FIREARM NAME:

FIREARM TYPE

☐ HANDGUN   ☐ SHOTGUN   ☐ AIR GUN   ☐ SMG

☐ RIFLE   ☐ PISTOL   ☐ OTHER _____

SERIAL NUMBER		MANUFACTURER	
MODEL / TYPE		CALIBER	
WEIGHT		CAPACITY	
BARREL LENGTH		BARREL TYPE	
ACTION		IDENTIFIERS	
ALTERATIONS		OTHER NOTES	
REPAIRS			

ACQUISITION & DISPOSITION INFORMATION

PURCHASED FROM		DATE	
ADDRESS			
ID NUMBER		DOB	
CONDITION		PRICE	
PURCHASE DETAILS			

SOLD TO		DATE	
ADDRESS			
ID NUMBER		DOB	
CONDITION		PRICE	
SALE DETAILS			

OTHER NOTES	

FIREARM NAME:

FIREARM TYPE

☐ HANDGUN	☐ SHOTGUN	☐ AIR GUN	☐ SMG
☐ RIFLE	☐ PISTOL	☐ OTHER _____	

SERIAL NUMBER		MANUFACTURER	
MODEL / TYPE		CALIBER	
WEIGHT		CAPACITY	
BARREL LENGTH		BARREL TYPE	
ACTION		IDENTIFIERS	
ALTERATIONS		OTHER NOTES	
REPAIRS			

ACQUISITION & DISPOSITION INFORMATION

PURCHASED FROM		DATE	
ADDRESS			
ID NUMBER		DOB	
CONDITION		PRICE	
PURCHASE DETAILS			

SOLD TO		DATE	
ADDRESS			
ID NUMBER		DOB	
CONDITION		PRICE	
SALE DETAILS			

OTHER NOTES	

FIREARM NAME:	33

FIREARM TYPE

☐ HANDGUN	☐ SHOTGUN	☐ AIR GUN	☐ SMG
☐ RIFLE	☐ PISTOL	☐ OTHER _____	

SERIAL NUMBER		**MANUFACTURER**	
MODEL / TYPE		**CALIBER**	
WEIGHT		**CAPACITY**	
BARREL LENGTH		**BARREL TYPE**	
ACTION		**IDENTIFIERS**	
ALTERATIONS		**OTHER NOTES**	
REPAIRS			

ACQUISITION & DISPOSITION INFORMATION

PURCHASED FROM		DATE	
ADDRESS			
ID NUMBER		DOB	
CONDITION		PRICE	
PURCHASE DETAILS			

SOLD TO		DATE	
ADDRESS			
ID NUMBER		DOB	
CONDITION		PRICE	
SALE DETAILS			

OTHER NOTES	

FIREARM NAME:

34

FIREARM TYPE

| ☐ HANDGUN | ☐ SHOTGUN | ☐ AIR GUN | ☐ SMG |
| ☐ RIFLE | ☐ PISTOL | ☐ OTHER _____ | |

SERIAL NUMBER		MANUFACTURER	
MODEL / TYPE		CALIBER	
WEIGHT		CAPACITY	
BARREL LENGTH		BARREL TYPE	
ACTION		IDENTIFIERS	
ALTERATIONS		OTHER NOTES	
REPAIRS			

📷

ACQUISITION & DISPOSITION INFORMATION

PURCHASED FROM		DATE	
ADDRESS			
ID NUMBER		DOB	
CONDITION		PRICE	
PURCHASE DETAILS			

SOLD TO		DATE	
ADDRESS			
ID NUMBER		DOB	
CONDITION		PRICE	
SALE DETAILS			

OTHER NOTES	

FIREARM NAME: 35

FIREARM TYPE			
☐ HANDGUN	☐ SHOTGUN	☐ AIR GUN	☐ SMG
☐ RIFLE	☐ PISTOL	☐ OTHER _____	

SERIAL NUMBER		MANUFACTURER	
MODEL / TYPE		CALIBER	
WEIGHT		CAPACITY	
BARREL LENGTH		BARREL TYPE	
ACTION		IDENTIFIERS	
ALTERATIONS		OTHER NOTES	
REPAIRS			

ACQUISITION & DISPOSITION INFORMATION

PURCHASED FROM		DATE	
ADDRESS			
ID NUMBER		DOB	
CONDITION		PRICE	
PURCHASE DETAILS			

SOLD TO		DATE	
ADDRESS			
ID NUMBER		DOB	
CONDITION		PRICE	
SALE DETAILS			

OTHER NOTES	

FIREARM NAME:	36

FIREARM TYPE			
☐ HANDGUN	☐ SHOTGUN	☐ AIR GUN	☐ SMG
☐ RIFLE	☐ PISTOL	☐ OTHER _____	

SERIAL NUMBER		MANUFACTURER	
MODEL / TYPE		CALIBER	
WEIGHT		CAPACITY	
BARREL LENGTH		BARREL TYPE	
ACTION		IDENTIFIERS	
ALTERATIONS		OTHER NOTES	
REPAIRS			

ACQUISITION & DISPOSITION INFORMATION

PURCHASED FROM		DATE	
ADDRESS			
ID NUMBER		DOB	
CONDITION		PRICE	
PURCHASE DETAILS			

SOLD TO		DATE	
ADDRESS			
ID NUMBER		DOB	
CONDITION		PRICE	
SALE DETAILS			

OTHER NOTES	

FIREARM NAME: | 37

FIREARM TYPE

- ☐ HANDGUN
- ☐ RIFLE
- ☐ SHOTGUN
- ☐ PISTOL
- ☐ AIR GUN
- ☐ OTHER _____
- ☐ SMG

SERIAL NUMBER		**MANUFACTURER**	
MODEL / TYPE		**CALIBER**	
WEIGHT		**CAPACITY**	
BARREL LENGTH		**BARREL TYPE**	
ACTION		**IDENTIFIERS**	
ALTERATIONS		**OTHER NOTES**	
REPAIRS			

ACQUISITION & DISPOSITION INFORMATION

PURCHASED FROM		DATE	
ADDRESS			
ID NUMBER		DOB	
CONDITION		PRICE	
PURCHASE DETAILS			

SOLD TO		DATE	
ADDRESS			
ID NUMBER		DOB	
CONDITION		PRICE	
SALE DETAILS			

OTHER NOTES	

FIREARM NAME:

38

FIREARM TYPE			
☐ HANDGUN	☐ SHOTGUN	☐ AIR GUN	☐ SMG
☐ RIFLE	☐ PISTOL	☐ OTHER _____	

SERIAL NUMBER		MANUFACTURER	
MODEL / TYPE		CALIBER	
WEIGHT		CAPACITY	
BARREL LENGTH		BARREL TYPE	
ACTION		IDENTIFIERS	
ALTERATIONS		OTHER NOTES	
REPAIRS			

ACQUISITION & DISPOSITION INFORMATION

PURCHASED FROM		DATE	
ADDRESS			
ID NUMBER		DOB	
CONDITION		PRICE	
PURCHASE DETAILS			

SOLD TO		DATE	
ADDRESS			
ID NUMBER		DOB	
CONDITION		PRICE	
SALE DETAILS			

OTHER NOTES	

FIREARM NAME:

39

FIREARM TYPE

- ☐ HANDGUN
- ☐ RIFLE
- ☐ SHOTGUN
- ☐ PISTOL
- ☐ AIR GUN
- ☐ OTHER _____
- ☐ SMG

SERIAL NUMBER		MANUFACTURER	
MODEL / TYPE		CALIBER	
WEIGHT		CAPACITY	
BARREL LENGTH		BARREL TYPE	
ACTION		IDENTIFIERS	
ALTERATIONS		OTHER NOTES	
REPAIRS			

ACQUISITION & DISPOSITION INFORMATION

PURCHASED FROM		DATE	
ADDRESS			
ID NUMBER		DOB	
CONDITION		PRICE	
PURCHASE DETAILS			

SOLD TO		DATE	
ADDRESS			
ID NUMBER		DOB	
CONDITION		PRICE	
SALE DETAILS			

OTHER NOTES	

FIREARM NAME:

40

FIREARM TYPE

☐ HANDGUN ☐ SHOTGUN ☐ AIR GUN ☐ SMG

☐ RIFLE ☐ PISTOL ☐ OTHER _____

SERIAL NUMBER		**MANUFACTURER**	
MODEL / TYPE		**CALIBER**	
WEIGHT		**CAPACITY**	
BARREL LENGTH		**BARREL TYPE**	
ACTION		**IDENTIFIERS**	
ALTERATIONS		**OTHER NOTES**	
REPAIRS			

ACQUISITION & DISPOSITION INFORMATION

PURCHASED FROM		DATE	
ADDRESS			
ID NUMBER		DOB	
CONDITION		PRICE	
PURCHASE DETAILS			

SOLD TO		DATE	
ADDRESS			
ID NUMBER		DOB	
CONDITION		PRICE	
SALE DETAILS			

OTHER NOTES	

FIREARM NAME:

41

FIREARM TYPE

☐ HANDGUN	☐ SHOTGUN	☐ AIR GUN	☐ SMG
☐ RIFLE	☐ PISTOL	☐ OTHER _____	

SERIAL NUMBER		**MANUFACTURER**	
MODEL / TYPE		**CALIBER**	.
WEIGHT		**CAPACITY**	
BARREL LENGTH		**BARREL TYPE**	
ACTION		**IDENTIFIERS**	
ALTERATIONS		**OTHER NOTES**	
REPAIRS			

ACQUISITION & DISPOSITION INFORMATION

PURCHASED FROM		DATE	
ADDRESS			
ID NUMBER		DOB	
CONDITION		PRICE	
PURCHASE DETAILS			

SOLD TO		DATE	
ADDRESS			
ID NUMBER		DOB	
CONDITION		PRICE	
SALE DETAILS			

OTHER NOTES	

FIREARM NAME:

FIREARM TYPE

☐ HANDGUN ☐ SHOTGUN ☐ AIR GUN ☐ SMG

☐ RIFLE ☐ PISTOL ☐ OTHER _____

SERIAL NUMBER		MANUFACTURER	
MODEL / TYPE		CALIBER	
WEIGHT		CAPACITY	
BARREL LENGTH		BARREL TYPE	
ACTION		IDENTIFIERS	
ALTERATIONS		OTHER NOTES	
REPAIRS			

ACQUISITION & DISPOSITION INFORMATION

PURCHASED FROM		DATE	
ADDRESS			
ID NUMBER		DOB	
CONDITION		PRICE	
PURCHASE DETAILS			

SOLD TO		DATE	
ADDRESS			
ID NUMBER		DOB	
CONDITION		PRICE	
SALE DETAILS			

OTHER NOTES	

FIREARM NAME: 43

FIREARM TYPE

- ☐ HANDGUN
- ☐ RIFLE
- ☐ SHOTGUN
- ☐ PISTOL
- ☐ AIR GUN
- ☐ OTHER _____
- ☐ SMG

SERIAL NUMBER		MANUFACTURER	
MODEL / TYPE		CALIBER	
WEIGHT		CAPACITY	
BARREL LENGTH		BARREL TYPE	
ACTION		IDENTIFIERS	
ALTERATIONS		OTHER NOTES	
REPAIRS			

ACQUISITION & DISPOSITION INFORMATION

PURCHASED FROM		DATE	
ADDRESS			
ID NUMBER		DOB	
CONDITION		PRICE	
PURCHASE DETAILS			

SOLD TO		DATE	
ADDRESS			
ID NUMBER		DOB	
CONDITION		PRICE	
SALE DETAILS			

OTHER NOTES	

FIREARM NAME: | 44

FIREARM TYPE			
☐ HANDGUN	☐ SHOTGUN	☐ AIR GUN	☐ SMG
☐ RIFLE	☐ PISTOL	☐ OTHER _____	

SERIAL NUMBER		MANUFACTURER	
MODEL / TYPE		CALIBER	
WEIGHT		CAPACITY	
BARREL LENGTH		BARREL TYPE	
ACTION		IDENTIFIERS	
ALTERATIONS		OTHER NOTES	
REPAIRS			

ACQUISITION & DISPOSITION INFORMATION

PURCHASED FROM		DATE	
ADDRESS			
ID NUMBER		DOB	
CONDITION		PRICE	
PURCHASE DETAILS			

SOLD TO		DATE	
ADDRESS			
ID NUMBER		DOB	
CONDITION		PRICE	
SALE DETAILS			

OTHER NOTES	

FIREARM NAME: 45

FIREARM TYPE			
☐ HANDGUN	☐ SHOTGUN	☐ AIR GUN	☐ SMG
☐ RIFLE	☐ PISTOL	☐ OTHER _____	

SERIAL NUMBER		**MANUFACTURER**	
MODEL / TYPE		**CALIBER**	
WEIGHT		**CAPACITY**	
BARREL LENGTH		**BARREL TYPE**	
ACTION		**IDENTIFIERS**	
ALTERATIONS		**OTHER NOTES**	
REPAIRS			

ACQUISITION & DISPOSITION INFORMATION

PURCHASED FROM		DATE	
ADDRESS			
ID NUMBER		DOB	
CONDITION		PRICE	
PURCHASE DETAILS			

SOLD TO		DATE	
ADDRESS			
ID NUMBER		DOB	
CONDITION		PRICE	
SALE DETAILS			

OTHER NOTES	

FIREARM NAME:

FIREARM TYPE

☐ HANDGUN	☐ SHOTGUN	☐ AIR GUN	☐ SMG
☐ RIFLE	☐ PISTOL	☐ OTHER _____	

SERIAL NUMBER		MANUFACTURER	
MODEL / TYPE		CALIBER	
WEIGHT		CAPACITY	
BARREL LENGTH		BARREL TYPE	
ACTION		IDENTIFIERS	
ALTERATIONS		OTHER NOTES	
REPAIRS			

ACQUISITION & DISPOSITION INFORMATION

PURCHASED FROM		DATE	
ADDRESS			
ID NUMBER		DOB	
CONDITION		PRICE	
PURCHASE DETAILS			

SOLD TO		DATE	
ADDRESS			
ID NUMBER		DOB	
CONDITION		PRICE	
SALE DETAILS			

OTHER NOTES	

FIREARM NAME: | 47

FIREARM TYPE			
☐ HANDGUN	☐ SHOTGUN	☐ AIR GUN	☐ SMG
☐ RIFLE	☐ PISTOL	☐ OTHER _____	

SERIAL NUMBER		MANUFACTURER	
MODEL / TYPE		CALIBER	
WEIGHT		CAPACITY	
BARREL LENGTH		BARREL TYPE	
ACTION		IDENTIFIERS	
ALTERATIONS		OTHER NOTES	
REPAIRS			

ACQUISITION & DISPOSITION INFORMATION

PURCHASED FROM		DATE	
ADDRESS			
ID NUMBER		DOB	
CONDITION		PRICE	
PURCHASE DETAILS			

SOLD TO		DATE	
ADDRESS			
ID NUMBER		DOB	
CONDITION		PRICE	
SALE DETAILS			

OTHER NOTES	

FIREARM NAME:

48

FIREARM TYPE			
☐ HANDGUN	☐ SHOTGUN	☐ AIR GUN	☐ SMG
☐ RIFLE	☐ PISTOL	☐ OTHER _____	

SERIAL NUMBER		**MANUFACTURER**	
MODEL / TYPE		**CALIBER**	
WEIGHT		**CAPACITY**	
BARREL LENGTH		**BARREL TYPE**	
ACTION		**IDENTIFIERS**	
ALTERATIONS		**OTHER NOTES**	
REPAIRS			

ACQUISITION & DISPOSITION INFORMATION

PURCHASED FROM		DATE	
ADDRESS			
ID NUMBER		DOB	
CONDITION		PRICE	
PURCHASE DETAILS			

SOLD TO		DATE	
ADDRESS			
ID NUMBER		DOB	
CONDITION		PRICE	
SALE DETAILS			

OTHER NOTES	

FIREARM NAME:

49

FIREARM TYPE

- ☐ HANDGUN
- ☐ RIFLE
- ☐ SHOTGUN
- ☐ PISTOL
- ☐ AIR GUN
- ☐ OTHER _____
- ☐ SMG

SERIAL NUMBER		**MANUFACTURER**	
MODEL / TYPE		**CALIBER**	
WEIGHT		**CAPACITY**	
BARREL LENGTH		**BARREL TYPE**	
ACTION		**IDENTIFIERS**	
ALTERATIONS		**OTHER NOTES**	
REPAIRS			

ACQUISITION & DISPOSITION INFORMATION

PURCHASED FROM		DATE	
ADDRESS			
ID NUMBER		DOB	
CONDITION		PRICE	
PURCHASE DETAILS			

SOLD TO		DATE	
ADDRESS			
ID NUMBER		DOB	
CONDITION		PRICE	
SALE DETAILS			

OTHER NOTES	

FIREARM NAME:

50

FIREARM TYPE			
☐ HANDGUN	☐ SHOTGUN	☐ AIR GUN	☐ SMG
☐ RIFLE	☐ PISTOL	☐ OTHER _____	

SERIAL NUMBER		**MANUFACTURER**	
MODEL / TYPE		**CALIBER**	
WEIGHT		**CAPACITY**	
BARREL LENGTH		**BARREL TYPE**	
ACTION		**IDENTIFIERS**	
ALTERATIONS		**OTHER NOTES**	
REPAIRS			

ACQUISITION & DISPOSITION INFORMATION

PURCHASED FROM		DATE	
ADDRESS			
ID NUMBER		DOB	
CONDITION		PRICE	
PURCHASE DETAILS			

SOLD TO		DATE	
ADDRESS			
ID NUMBER		DOB	
CONDITION		PRICE	
SALE DETAILS			

OTHER NOTES	